ABIGAIL SKERRITT-JONES

Florida Couples Adventure

100 Budget-Friendly Attractions, Activities, and Restaurants for Two

To Frank and Joanne, a couple whose love story has been an inspiration and a testament to the enduring magic of shared adventures. Your steadfast dedication to cherishing love and embracing the beauty of life together has guided and inspired many along their own paths. Here's to Frank and Joanne, whose love is a beacon for all of us on this Florida Couples Adventure.

Contents

Preface

⚜

Welcome to the enchanting world of budget-friendly adventures for couples in the Sunshine State. As an author, I've had the privilege of exploring Florida's diverse landscapes and coastal wonders, and I'm thrilled to be your guide on this journey to discovering romance, adventure, and connection without breaking the bank.In the face of the ongoing financial challenges in Florida, characterized by rising taxes, escalating rent, and soaring food prices, it becomes increasingly vital for couples to come together and prioritize their relationships. Economic pressures can significantly strain individuals and families, but amidst these hardships, carving out time for meaningful togetherness serves as a beacon of strength and resilience. By reaffirming their bonds and focusing on shared experiences, couples not only weather the financial storms but also find solace and support in each other, ultimately fortifying their relationships against the trials of these uncertain times.

Florida, with its endless stretches of pristine beaches, lush natural beauty, and vibrant cities, offers an array of opportunities for couples to create lasting memories together. Whether you're seeking a serene sunset walk along the shoreline, an adrenaline-pumping adventure, or a taste of local culture and cuisine, this book is your passport to affordable yet unforgettable experiences.

But it's more than just a collection of activities; it's an invitation to reignite the spark of romance and embark on new adventures hand in hand. It's about stepping out of your comfort zone, trying new things, and, most importantly, deepening your connection and communication with your partner. In the hustle and bustle of everyday life, we often forget the joy of discovery, the thrill of shared experiences, and the power of open, heartfelt conversations.

Do not feel confined to the suggested cities. Some lesser-known towns offer similar experiences and are just as economical. We have included some websites and addresses for many specific adventures that are worth crossing off your bucket list.

The beauty of these activities lies not only in their affordability but also in their ability to deepen your connection as a couple. As you try new things together—whether paddleboarding on the Intracoastal, building intricate sandcastles, or sharing an ice cream cone—you'll discover new facets of each other and strengthen the bonds of your relationship.

Our hope is that these adventures will not only bring you closer but also remind you of the simple yet profound joys of love and togetherness. As you explore Florida's coastal gems, take in the breathtaking scenery, and embrace the thrill of new experiences, remember to savor each moment, cherish your time together, and let the romance of the Sunshine State weave its magic into your relationship.

Let's dive in and explore the budget-friendly activities that will make your Florida getaway a true celebration of love and adventure.

Abigail Skerritt-Jones

One

Crafted Creations

Photo by vishnudeep dixit: https://www.pexels.com/photo/grayscale-photo-of-couple-walking-on-seashore-1260802/

In the 'Crafted Creations' section of this adventure guide, we invite couples to embark on a journey of exploration, creativity, and connection. Here, you'll find inspiration on how to collect and craft mementos that encapsulate the beauty and romance of your seaside experiences. From gathering seashells along the shore to designing personalized beach glass jewelry, we'll briefly show you how to turn your love for the ocean into tangible memories. Discover the art of driftwood creations and the sentimental power of messages in bottles. Whether filling sand jars with the essence of your favorite beach or sketching the breathtaking seascapes you encounter, 'Crafted Creations' is your gateway to immortalizing the magic of coastal adventures and weaving the tapestry of your shared love story with the sea.

Here are 10 Keepsakes you can collect or make from ocean adventures to cherish your experiences. These mementos, be they collectibles of natural beauty or heartfelt creations from your own hand, are designed to help you cherish your experiences on the open sea, preserving the magic of the waves, the whispers of the shoreline, and the stories of your nautical escapades for years to come.

Certainly! Here are expanded descriptions for each creative beach-inspired activity:

1. Seashell Collection:
   - Gather a wide array of seashells during your beach visits, each one unique in shape, size, and color. Create a visually stunning

and personalized collection by arranging them in a decorative jar. Alternatively, use the seashells to craft canvas art, incorporating sand for texture, or arrange them creatively around a picture frame, turning your seaside treasures into a beautiful reminder of your coastal explorations.

2. Beach Glass Jewelry:
   - Embrace the allure of smooth, frosted beach glass by turning these treasures into wearable art. Collect pieces in various shades and shapes, then transform them into custom jewelry such as necklaces or bracelets. Each piece of jewelry will carry with it the essence of the ocean, serving as a tangible reminder of your time spent by the sea.

3. Driftwood Art:
   - Explore the shoreline for pieces of weathered driftwood and channel your creativity into crafting unique art or decor items. Consider making picture frames, mirrors, or candle holders using the collected driftwood. Personalize each piece to reflect your love for the sea, whether it's through intricate carvings, paint, or additional beach-themed embellishments.

4. Sand Jar:
   - Capture the essence of your favorite beach by filling a decorative jar with its sand. Label the jar with the location and date, creating a visually pleasing and sentimental reminder of your ocean adventures. Display the sand jar in your home, allowing it to evoke the sights, sounds, and memories of your cherished beach moments.

5. Customized Seashell Candles:
   - Infuse a touch of coastal charm into your home by creating customized candles adorned with embedded seashells. As the candles burn, the seashells will be gradually revealed, making each candle a

unique keepsake. Choose scents that evoke the ocean breeze, creating a sensory experience that transports you back to the seaside.

6. Beach Photo Album:
   - Compile the snapshots of your ocean adventures into a personalized photo album. Add captions, notes, and anecdotes to each picture, capturing the emotions and stories behind the moments you've shared. Your beach photo album will become a cherished visual narrative of your love's journey by the sea.

7. Message in a Bottle:
   - Add a touch of romance to your beach visits by writing heartfelt messages to each other and sealing them in a glass bottle. Toss the bottle into the sea, allowing it to drift and wash ashore, creating a whimsical and symbolic gesture of your love's journey. Alternatively, keep the bottle as a unique decoration and a reminder of your shared sentiments.

8. Beach Sketchbook:
   - Carry a dedicated beach sketchbook during your coastal escapades. Sketch the scenic landscapes, seascapes, or even each other as you relax by the water. Over time, your sketchbook will become a captivating visual journal, capturing the beauty and tranquility of your beach experiences through your artistic interpretations.

9. Customized Beach Towels:
   - Elevate your beach outings by designing customized beach towels featuring your names, special dates, or a favorite beach quote. These towels serve as practical and stylish accessories while also preserving the memories of your seaside adventures. Choose vibrant colors and durable materials for a perfect blend of function and sentiment.

10. Sea Glass Wind Chimes:
  - Craft a charming wind chime using collected sea glass, driftwood, and shells. Arrange the sea glass in a cascading pattern, allowing it to catch the sunlight and create a mesmerizing display of colors. Hang the wind chime on your porch or in your garden, bringing the soothing sounds of the sea breeze to your home. This DIY project adds a touch of coastal serenity to your outdoor spaces.

These mementos preserve the memories of your ocean adventures and serve as beautiful reminders of your connection and shared experiences.

Two

Beachside Bliss

Photo by Gusti Mega: https://www.pexels.com/photo/a-photo-of-a-man-carrying-woman-on-the-beach-9317167/

As the sun kisses the horizon and the waves serenade the shore, we invite you to embark on a journey of love and connection with beachside activities in the enchanting state of Florida. In this chapter, we explore the harmonious dance between couples and the captivating coastal beauty that sets the stage for unforgettable moments.

Florida's sun-soaked beaches provide the canvas for an array of activities that go beyond the ordinary. From the Atlantic's rhythmic waves to the Gulf Coast's gentle embrace, couples are invited to immerse themselves in a symphony of sensations. Picture yourselves strolling hand in hand along the sandy shores, the salty breeze carrying whispers of adventure and romance.

Join us as we uncover the magic of sunrise and sunset beach walks, where the sky transforms into a canvas of hues, painting the perfect backdrop for quiet conversations and stolen kisses. Dive into the joy of beach picnics, where the simplicity of a blanket and a shared meal becomes a celebration of love against the soothing soundtrack of the ocean's melody.

But the journey doesn't end there. Challenge each other to a spirited game of beach volleyball, feel the excitement of stand-up paddleboarding, or paddle together on the tranquil waters of the Intracoastal, exploring mangrove forests hand in hand. Each activity becomes a brushstroke in the masterpiece of your shared experiences.

As you read on, envision building sandcastles together, discovering seashells that tell stories of the ocean's secrets, and capturing the beauty of your time with beach photography. From thrilling adventures to serene moments, every page of this chapter invites you to create a symphony of love by the sea, weaving precious memories that will linger like the scent of salt in the air.

So, dear readers, let the tide of inspiration guide you as we delve into the vibrant world of beachside activities in Florida—a chapter where the sea becomes not just a backdrop but an active participant in the love story you continue to write together.

1. Sunrise Beach Walks -*Recommended City: Any coastal city in Florida*
Picture this: you and your partner, strolling along the shoreline at the break of day, ready to embrace the pure magic of a Florida sunrise. As you amble along, the sky starts its mesmerizing transformation into a canvas of vibrant colors. It's like nature itself is putting on a show just for the two of you. Hues of orange, pink, and gold intermingle in a breathtaking display, casting a warm and inviting glow on your surroundings.

And then there's the soundtrack, a symphony conducted by the gentle waves. Their rhythm, like a soothing lullaby, serenades your senses, creating an enchanting atmosphere that's hard to put into words. It's as though the world has hushed to let you and your partner connect on a deeper level, sharing your thoughts, your dreams, and your stories.

Whether you are early risers or prefer the warmth of a sunset, these beach walks offer a backdrop that's like no other. They set the stage for meaningful conversations and connections that are etched into your memories. It's nature's way of saying, "Here's a canvas of beauty, now go create your masterpiece of love."

2. Sunset Beach Walks -*Recommended City: Any West Coast city in Florida*

Sunset beach walks in Florida epitomize the essence of romance, forging connections that transcend personal boundaries and time itself. As the radiant sun embarks on its slow descent below the horizon, it bequeaths the sky with a mesmerizing symphony of warm colors. This masterpiece becomes the canvas for lovers meandering along the shoreline. The shifting hues of gold, pink, and tangerine fuse with the deepening blues, creating a breathtaking, ever-changing backdrop that mirrors the kaleidoscope of emotions shared by couples on this tranquil journey.

The soothing rhythm of the waves, like a natural lullaby, accompanies your footsteps, orchestrating the perfect soundtrack for your shared adventure. Each footfall on the soft, grainy sand is a reminder of the steady march of time, but it's also a testament to the enduring bond between you and your partner. The world around you seems to hush, inviting you to speak from the heart and listen with intent. It's a canvas upon which you can paint your dreams, share your aspirations, and reminisce about your shared history.

Whether you choose to greet the day with a dawn beach walk or bid it adieu with a sunset stroll, the beauty of the coastal landscape is a constant companion, a steadfast witness to your love story. These moments by the shore allow you to lose yourselves in the vastness of the sea and sky, offering a profound sense of perspective and the chance to reflect on the vastness of your shared journey. The memories you create during these beach walks are etched into the sands of time, leaving an indelible mark on your hearts and a testament to the enduring love that finds its home in the embrace of Florida's coastal splendor.

3. Beach Picnics -*Recommended City: Any coastal city in Florida*

Create a truly romantic escapade by orchestrating a picnic affair that transcends the ordinary. Begin by meticulously selecting an array of your most cherished snacks, preparing delectable sandwiches, and chilling your preferred beverages. As you pack these delights into a well-appointed picnic basket, you'll infuse the act with anticipation and thoughtfulness, setting the stage for an exceptional outing.

With your provisions in hand, venture to the beach, where the allure of the coastal landscape awaits. Find a secluded nook where the sands stretch out to meet the gentle lull of the sea, and there, lay down a comfortable, inviting blanket. The soft, golden grains provide a natural canvas for your impromptu feast.

As you settle in with your partner, the ocean's symphony of waves serves as your serenade, creating an enchanting ambiance for your shared meal. The briny scent in the air, the seagulls' gentle calls, and the cool breeze all contribute to the sense of being enveloped in nature's embrace. This intimate rendezvous allows you to relish each other's company amidst the unspoiled beauty of the coast. The act of sharing a simple, yet thoughtfully prepared meal, combined with the backdrop of the vast, boundless ocean, elevates this experience into an unforgettable memory of love and togetherness.

4. Beach Volleyball- *Recommended Cities: Miami Beach, Clearwater Beach, Fort Lauderdale, etc.*

Infuse some fun and friendly competition into your beach day by challenging each other to a game of beach volleyball. Most popular Florida beaches have designated courts or nets, providing the ideal setting for active couples to enjoy some spirited matches. Whether you're a seasoned player or a beginner, beach volleyball promises laughter, teamwork, and a memorable time.

Photo by Yelena Odintsova: https://www.pexels.com/photo/people-horseback-riding-on-the-beach-16197832/

5. Horseback Riding on the Beach- *Recommended Cities: Amelia Island, Cape San Blas, Hutchinson Island, Fort Pierce, etc.*
Discover the sheer joy of exploring the coastline on horseback with your partner. Many coastal destinations in Florida offer guided horseback riding experiences along pristine shores. As you and your partner ride gracefully along the beach, you'll be captivated by the rhythmic sound of hooves meeting the sand and the breathtaking ocean views stretching to the horizon. It's a romantic and adventurous way to connect with both nature and each other. This is one of my favorite Florida adventures.
http://www.beachtoursonhorseback.com/
$50 for a 1-hour ride.

6. Kayaking on the Intracoastal- *Recommended Cities: St. Augustine, Fort Lauderdale, Sarasota, etc.*
Rent a tandem kayak and embark on a serene paddling adventure on the peaceful waters of the Intracoastal Waterway. As you navigate through mangrove forests, observe local wildlife, and savor the serenity of the coastal ecosystem, you and your partner can create lasting

memories in a tranquil, natural setting. It's an intimate and eco-friendly way to explore Florida's hidden gems.

https://kayakingsrq.com/kayaking-tours/

Sarasota Kayaking Tours- Starting at $59

Photo by Lucas Andreatta:
https://www.pexels.com/photo/surfers-with-surfboards-13347792/

7. Stand-Up Paddleboarding (SUP)- *Recommended Cities: Daytona Beach, Sarasota, Key West, etc.*

Try your hand at stand-up paddleboarding for a unique and exciting adventure. Rent paddleboards and explore the calm waters of the Intracoastal while testing your balance and teamwork. Glide along the water's surface, enjoying the scenic views and creating unforgettable moments with your partner. Paddleboarding is just one of many watersports you can try. If this is not to your fancy, explore others like surfing or snorkeling.

https://paddleboardingpalmbeach.com/

Varying Tours-Starting at $75

8. Sandcastle Building -*Recommended City: Any coastal city with sandy beaches*

Perhaps reliving memories of building sandcastles as a child, unleash your inner artist, and work together to build intricate and imaginative sandcastles on the beach. Mold and sculpt the soft, white sand into impressive creations, whether it's a majestic castle or a whimsical sculpture. This lighthearted and artistic activity encourages collaboration and playful creativity, all while appreciating the natural beauty of the beach. Glean inspiration from The Siesta Key Crystal Classic International Sand Sculpting Festival.

www.SiestaKeyCrystalClassic.com

Tickets start at $12

9. Beach Photography- *Recommended City: Any coastal city in Florida*

Capture the beauty of the beach and your time together with a beach photography session. Armed with your camera or smartphone, experiment with different angles and lighting to create lasting memories. Whether you're framing the sunrise, capturing candid moments, or exploring creative compositions, photography allows you to freeze time and cherish the essence of your coastal adventure together. It's a delightful way to document your journey and celebrate your connection.

16

10. Naturist Beach Experience -*Recommended Beach: Haulover Beach, Miami, FL*

For couples seeking a liberating and unique beach experience, Haulover Beach in Miami beckons with open arms. Located in sunny Florida, this clothing-optional beach allows you to embrace the freedom of nature in a respectful and accepting environment. As you venture to Haulover Beach, you will discover a community of like-minded individuals who share an appreciation for the beauty of the human form and the serenity of the ocean. Whether sunbathing, swimming, or simply enjoying a stroll along the shore, the absence of clothing fosters a sense of authenticity and a profound connection with the natural surroundings. It's an opportunity to shed inhibitions, bask in the warm Miami sun, and create unforgettable memories with your partner in a truly unique setting. Remember to respect the beach's guidelines and the privacy of fellow beachgoers, and you'll find that the Naturist Beach Experience can be a liberating and profoundly intimate way to connect as a couple.

https://www.miamidade.gov/parks/haulover.asp

*Photo by Soner Arkan: https://www.pexels.com/photo/a-man-jumping-into
-the-water-from-a-boat-18328135/*

11. Outdoor Movie Nights-*Recommended Cities: Hollywood Beach, Miami Beach, Pensacola etc.*

For a memorable and romantic evening, check local event listings for outdoor movie screenings on the beach. Grab a cozy blanket, snacks, and your partner's hand, and settle in for a cinematic experience under the starry Florida sky. With the gentle sound of the waves in the background and the ocean as your backdrop, it's an enchanting way to enjoy a film together in a unique setting.

12. Surfing Lessons-*Recommended Cities: Cocoa Beach, Jacksonville Beach, etc.*

If you're both up for an adventure, why not try your hand at surfing? Sign up for beginner surfing lessons and ride the waves together. Surfing provides an exhilarating and challenging experience that can help you bond as you learn the ropes. With skilled instructors guiding you, catching your first wave becomes a thrilling achievement to celebrate together.

www.getyourguide.com

19

13. Mini Golf-*Recommended City: Many coastal cities have mini golf courses*

Challenge each other to a lively round of mini golf at one of the many coastal courses in Florida. Navigate through whimsical obstacles and intricate putting greens, all while sharing laughter and friendly competition. Mini golf is a fun and playful way to spend quality time together, and it's an excellent choice for couples looking to enjoy some lighthearted entertainment.

14. Bird Watching-*Recommended Cities: Merritt Island, Fort Myers Beach, etc.*

Embrace the tranquility of bird watching as you bring binoculars and a bird guidebook to the beach. Spend your time identifying and observing the diverse bird species that call the coastline home. Whether spotting graceful shorebirds or colorful songbirds, bird watching allows you to appreciate the natural beauty and biodiversity of Florida's coastal areas while sharing a peaceful and educational activity. Take pictures and start a lifetime bird-sighting collection.

www.fws.gov/refuge/merritt-isla

Daily Pass is $10 per vehicle.

Photo by ArtHouse Studio: https://www.pexels.com/photo/grayscale-photo-of-couple-sitting-on-beach-shore-4514021/

15. Beach Bonfires

- *Recommended Cities: Some beaches permit bonfires with proper permits.*

If your chosen beach allows it with the appropriate permits, consider creating a cozy beach bonfire with your partner. Gather around the warm, crackling flames, roast marshmallows, and share stories under the starlit sky. The ambiance of a beach bonfire is incredibly romantic and provides the perfect setting for intimate conversations and quiet moments together.

16. Beachfront Ice Cream Date

- *Recommended City: Any coastal city with ice cream shops near the beach*

Indulge your sweet tooth with a delightful beachfront ice cream date. Visit a nearby ice cream shop to choose your favorite flavors, then enjoy your scoops while sitting by the water's edge. The combination of creamy treats and the cool ocean breeze provides a refreshing and sweet way to relax and connect.

17. Shell Island Exploration

• *Recommended City: Panama City Beach, Shell Island.*

Embark on a memorable adventure by renting a boat or kayak to visit Shell Island near Panama City Beach. This secluded and pristine island offers privacy, crystal-clear waters, and the opportunity to explore untouched natural surroundings. Discover hidden coves, go snorkeling, or simply relax on the sandy shores—it's an intimate and secluded escape for couples seeking serenity.
https://shellkeyshuttle.com/
Shuttle- $25
Ferry-$27.95

18. Visit Historic Piers

• *Recommended Cities: Cocoa Beach Pier, Naples Pier, etc.*

Enjoy a romantic stroll on historic piers like Cocoa Beach Pier or Naples Pier. Take in the refreshing ocean breeze, stunning views of the coastline, and perhaps some local entertainment. Piers provide a charming setting for couples to connect, watch the waves, and share the timeless beauty of the sea.

19. Beachcomber's Paradise

- *Recommended Cities: Sanibel Island, Captiva Island*

Head to Sanibel Island or Captiva Island, which are renowned for their extensive seashell deposits. Spend hours beachcombing and collecting unique shells that wash ashore. The tranquil atmosphere of these islands invites you to explore the sandy shores and appreciate the natural treasures that the ocean offers. It's a relaxing and meditative activity perfect for couples.

20. Sailboat Rides

* *Recommended Cities: St. Petersburg, Sarasota, Stuart.*

Set sail on an affordable sailing tour along the Intracoastal Waterway. Feel the wind in your hair and the sense of adventure as you and your partner navigate the beautiful coastal scenery together. Whether you're helping to hoist the sails or simply enjoying the serenity of the water, sailing provides an idyllic setting for connection and relaxation, making it a memorable experience for couples.

https://www.treasurecoastsailingadventures.com/
Starting at $60

Three

Outdoor Odysseys

Photo by Jonathan Borba: https://www.pexels.com/photo/smiling-couple-on
-old-bridge-above-grass-7486319/

Welcome to a chapter where the great outdoors becomes the canvas for your shared adventures, where the vibrant landscapes of Florida unfold as the backdrop to your love story. From the lush greenery of state parks to the meandering rivers and the welcoming embrace of sun-dappled trails, this chapter invites you to immerse yourselves in the heart of nature, hand in hand.

Florida's diverse ecosystems provide the stage for an array of outdoor activities that promise to elevate your connection. Whether you find solace in the rustling palms, the calls of exotic birds, or the gentle lapping of water against the shore, the outdoor spaces in Florida beckon couples to create memories that resonate with the rhythm of nature.

Imagine embarking on hiking trails that lead to hidden waterfalls, kayaking adventures along meandering rivers, or cycling through canopies of ancient oaks. Nature becomes your accomplice in discovering not just the beauty of the state but also the joy of exploration and togetherness.

In this chapter, we explore the thrill of seeking the unknown together. From the adrenaline rush of ziplining through lush canopies to the tranquility of bird-watching in secluded parks, every page is an invitation to escape the ordinary and revel in the extraordinary moments nature has to offer.

As you read on, envision the sun's warm embrace as you navigate through nature trails, the refreshing mist of waterfalls on your faces, and the shared laughter echoing through the forests. Each outdoor activity becomes a celebration of your connection, a reminder that love is not just nurtured in intimate moments but flourishes in the open spaces where adventure and serenity coexist.

So, dear readers, let this chapter be your guide to the outdoor wonders of Florida—a tale of shared exploration, discovery, and the pure joy that comes from basking in the beauty of nature together. Nature's embrace awaits, promising a chapter rich with outdoor bliss and memories etched in the heart of the Sunshine State.

1. Airboat Tours in the Everglades-*Recommended Cities*: Miami, Fort Lauderdale, Naples
Hold tight as you embark on an unforgettable airboat tour through the vast and mysterious Everglades. Feel the exhilaration as the boat glides over the water, propelled by a powerful fan. You and your partner will have a front-row seat to witness the incredible wildlife that calls this unique ecosystem home, including alligators, turtles, and exotic birds. The rush of the wind and the thrill of the adventure make this an ideal activity for couples seeking an adrenaline boost.
www.gatorpark.com
Starting at $27.99

2. Ziplining Adventures-*Recommended Cities*: Ocala, Orlando, Brooksville
Take your love to new heights with a ziplining adventure in Florida's lush forests. Strapped into a harness, you and your partner will soar through the treetops, experiencing the rush of adrenaline and the beauty

of nature simultaneously. Zip from platform to platform, taking in breathtaking views and creating lasting memories together. It's a heart-pounding experience that's perfect for thrill-seeking couples.

www.gatorland.com

$69.99 includes access to the entire Gatorland Park

3. Go-Kart Racing-*Recommended Cities*: Orlando, Tampa, Fort Lauderdale, Kissimmee

Rev your engines and challenge each other to a thrilling go-kart race. Whether you're a seasoned racer or a beginner, the competitive spirit and excitement of zooming around the track will make for an unforgettable date. Work on your driving skills, test your limits, and share plenty of laughs as you compete to see who's the speediest couple.

www.kissimmeegokarts.com

Starting at $24 for six laps

4. Indoor Skydiving-*Recommended Cities*: Orlando, Tampa, Fort Lauderdale

Experience the sensation of freefalling without jumping out of an airplane by trying indoor skydiving. In a vertical wind tunnel, you'll float on a cushion of air, defying gravity. This thrilling activity offers a unique opportunity to hold hands and fly together safely indoors. It's an adrenaline rush that will leave you both smiling from ear to ear.

www.iflyworld.com

Starting at $69

5. Rock Climbing-*Recommended Cities*: Miami, Tampa, Jacksonville, Oakland Park

Challenge your physical and mental strength as a couple with indoor rock climbing. Climb walls of varying difficulty levels and rely on each other for support and encouragement. Rock climbing is an excellent way to build trust, communication, and teamwork while experiencing an exciting adventure together.

www.projectrock.com

Day pass starting at $30

6. Swamp Buggy Eco-Tours-*Recommended City*: Naples, Chokoloskee
Explore the wild side of Florida's swamps and marshes by hopping on a swamp buggy. These rugged vehicles are designed to traverse the terrain, allowing you and your partner to get up close and personal with the region's unique wildlife, including alligators and wading birds. Your guide will share fascinating insights about the ecosystem, making it an educational and thrilling experience.
https://www.bigcypressswampbuggytours.com/
$140 for a 4-hour tour

7. Adventure Ropes Courses-*Recommended Cities*: St. Augustine, Orlando, Miami, Dade City
Test your courage and problem-solving skills on adventure ropes courses high above the ground. Navigate several obstacles, from wobbly bridges to swinging logs, while securely harnessed. Tackling these challenges together fosters teamwork, communication, and trust; the sense of accomplishment is incredibly rewarding.
https://treehoppers.com
Starting at $62.95 for three hours (book online to save $5)

Photo by Artem Podrez: https://www.pexels.com/photo/a-grayscale-photo-of-a-couple-with-horses-7986546/

8. Horseback Riding Trails-*Recommended Cities*: Ocala, Sarasota, Kissimmee

Experience the thrill of horseback riding on scenic trails that meander through Florida's forests, countryside, or even along the coastline. It's a romantic way to connect with nature and each other as you explore the great outdoors from the saddle. Whether you're both beginners or seasoned riders, it's an adventure that combines relaxation with excitement.

https://www.floridastateparks.org/parks-and-trails/lake-kissimmee-state-park

$5 Entrance fee per vehicle

9. Indoor Go-Kart Racing-*Recommended Cities*: Miami, Orlando, Tampa

If you prefer a climate-controlled environment, indoor go-kart racing is an excellent choice. Race against each other on professionally designed tracks, honing your driving skills and competing for the title of the fastest couple. The adrenaline rush of indoor karting ensures an action-packed date.

https://andrettikarting.com/orlando

Single race $27.95, Five Races $99.95

Photo by Tolga Aslantürk: https://www.pexels.com/photo/bride-and-groom-in-front-of-hot-air-balloon-14660133/

10. Hot Air Balloon Rides - *Recommended Cities*: Orlando, Kissimmee, Clermont –

Take your romance to new heights with a hot air balloon ride. Drift gracefully above the Florida landscape, enjoying panoramic views of forests, lakes, and scenic vistas. Whether you opt for a sunrise or sunset flight, the experience is both breathtaking and serene, offering a unique opportunity to connect with your partner and savor the beauty of the state from the sky. It's a memory you'll cherish forever.

https://www.airhoundfl.com

$275 per person on a shared ride.

$1850 Romantic ride for two

Four

Enchanting Evenings

Photo by cottonbro studio: https://www.pexels.com/photo/black-and-white-photo-of-a-couple-riding-a-bike-10071551/

This chapter includes questions couples can ask each other on a romantic night out to deepen their connection and create memorable conversations The essence of these inquiries lies in their power to spark meaningful conversations and reveal the intricacies of your partner's thoughts, feelings, and desires. As you delve into this section, you'll discover how these questions can serve as bridges between your hearts, fostering not only intimacy but also a treasure trove of cherished moments that will enrich your relationship.

1. Beach Bonfire - Destin, FL: Imagine this - you and your loved one, nestled on a sandy beach in beautiful Destin, FL, where the waves gently lap at the shore and stars twinkle above. Whether you're in the heart of a bustling city or a quieter coastal town, a beach bonfire is a truly magical and budget-friendly way to ignite the flames of romance. You'll find yourselves cozied up by the crackling fire, toasting marshmallows for s'mores, and letting the soothing sounds of the ocean waves serenade you. The simplicity and raw beauty of nature create an unparalleled backdrop, perfect for love to flourish. It's an unforgettable evening that blends the elements of earth, water, and fire, symbolizing the very essence of your connection.

What's your favorite memory from our time together, and why does it stand out to you?

2. Art Walk - St. Petersburg, FL: St. Petersburg's Art Walk beckons couples, offering a budget-friendly night out with an artistic twist, whether you're in a metropolis or a more intimate setting. This creative journey leads you through galleries, studios, and outdoor art displays, allowing you to soak in the vibrant local art scene. As you explore, your senses will be tantalized by the aroma of street food vendors offering delicious, yet affordable, bites. The streets come alive with live music and captivating street performances, adding to the artistic atmosphere. It's a date night that not only indulges your creative spirits but also supports local artists, making your connection even more meaningful.

If we could travel anywhere in the world together, where would you want to go and why?

3. Jazz Concerts at The Betsy - Miami Beach, FL: Miami Beach's The Betsy Hotel offers a romantic and budget-friendly experience that transcends city size. On its rooftop terrace, you'll be serenaded by complimentary jazz concerts set against the backdrop of breathtaking ocean views. This combination of smooth jazz melodies and the starlit canvas above creates an ambiance that speaks of love and elegance. Sip on cocktails or simply enjoy each other's company as the talented musicians provide the soundtrack to your evening. The twinkling Miami skyline and the tranquil ocean amplify the romantic atmosphere, ensuring an unforgettable night.

What's a dream or aspiration you have that you haven't shared with me yet?

4. Live Music at Tin Roof - Orlando, FL: Tin Roof in Orlando is the ultimate destination for music enthusiasts in both lively cities and smaller communities. What sets it apart is the absence of a cover charge, making it a budget-friendly option for couples seeking an evening of live music. Whether it's a local band showcasing their talent or a gifted solo artist, you can unwind in a casual and laid-back atmosphere. This provides the perfect backdrop to relax, chat, and bond over your shared passion for music. In this setting, your connection will harmonize with the melodies in the air.

What do you appreciate most about our relationship, and is there something you'd like us to work on or improve?

5. Sunset Celebration at Mallory Square - Key West, FL: The Sunset Celebration in Key West is a vibrant and budget-friendly experience that invites couples from all walks of life to partake in its unique charm. As the sun sets over the Gulf of Mexico, Key West's Mallory Square comes alive with local artists, street performers, and vendors displaying their crafts. It's a lively celebration of the city's culture and diversity, giving couples the opportunity to immerse themselves in the Key West experience without breaking the bank. As you watch the sun dip below the horizon, you'll be creating unforgettable memories, surrounded by the lively spirit of this unique destination.

If today were our last day together, how would you want to spend it, and what would you want me to know or remember?

*Photo by Polina Tankilevitch: https://www.pexels.com/photo/grayscale-phot
o-of-a-romantic-couple-hugging-7741742/*

6. Historic Ybor City - Tampa, FL: Tampa's historic Ybor City is a bustling district that comes to life as the night unfolds, offering budget-friendly bars, clubs, and restaurants for couples seeking a lively date night in a larger city. Roam the historic streets, where you can explore the rich heritage and architectural beauty of the area. Enjoy live music and savor affordable yet delightful meals and drinks. The lively atmosphere, combined with the charm of the city's architecture, provides an unforgettable backdrop for your evening. In Ybor City, you'll not only create memories but also immerse yourself in the vibrant local culture, enriching your connection.

What's a book, movie, or song that you feel deeply connected to, and how does it relate to your life or our relationship?

7. Boardwalk at Hollywood Beach - Hollywood, FL: Hollywood Beach's boardwalk is a versatile option for couples, regardless of whether they find themselves in a bustling metropolis or a quieter town. The boardwalk becomes a stage for free live music performances and street entertainment, allowing you to take a leisurely stroll by the beach while immersing yourselves in the vibrant atmosphere. While you meander, you can explore local shops and eateries, indulging in affordable yet

delightful bites. As you soak in the tranquil atmosphere and the beauty of the beach at night, you'll be creating an enchanting and romantic evening to remember.

What's one thing you've always wanted to learn or experience, and how can we work on achieving that together?

8. Free Outdoor Movies - Coral Gables, FL: Coral Gables extends an invitation to couples in both large cities and cozy towns to experience free outdoor movie nights, a charming and budget-friendly option. Picture yourself on a blanket under the starlit sky, your picnic basket brimming with your favorite snacks. This classic date night activity takes on a touch of old-school charm as you enjoy a cinematic adventure beneath the celestial canopy. It's a budget-friendly way to celebrate your love while relishing the magic of the silver screen.

Is there a small, everyday gesture or habit of mine that makes you feel loved and appreciated?

9. Open Mic Nights - Gainesville, FL: Gainesville's open mic nights create an affordable and engaging space for couples to experience local talent, whether you're in a bustling city or a smaller community. While you sip on a coffee or beverage of your choice, you'll be treated to live poetry readings, musical performances, and comedy acts. The intimate setting of cafes and bars provides a wonderful opportunity to bond over shared laughter, appreciation for the arts, and the talent of local performers. Your connection will grow stronger in this nurturing and creative environment.

What are your goals and priorities for the future, and how do you envision us working together to achieve them?

10. Downtown Riverwalk - Fort Lauderdale, FL: Fort Lauderdale's Downtown Riverwalk is a picturesque option that perfectly suits couples in large cities. Stroll along the scenic promenade, watch boats gliding by, and take in the captivating views of the city skyline illuminated at night. The Riverwalk frequently hosts free events, including outdoor concerts and art exhibitions, adding a cultural and budget-friendly dimension to your romantic evening. The tranquil waters and the soft glow of twinkling lights create a magical atmosphere, providing the ideal backdrop for couples to bond and cherish their connection. Whether you're celebrating a special occasion or simply enjoying quality time together, the Downtown Riverwalk offers a

unique and budget-friendly setting for love to flourish."

If you could describe our relationship in a single word or phrase, what would it be, and why does that word or phrase resonate with you?

Five

Wilderness Whispers

*Photo by Tamilles Esposito: https://www.pexels.com/photo/seagulls-flying-o
ver-sea-shore-in-black-and-white-18857138/*

In the heart of Florida's diverse landscapes lies a chapter waiting to be written—one that invites couples to step into the embrace of nature's wonders. This is a journey through the enchanting state parks, where towering palms sway, crystal-clear springs beckon, and the trails unfold like pages in a storybook of outdoor romance.

Welcome to a chapter where the rhythm of your footsteps becomes a symphony with nature's melodies, and the rustle of leaves and the calls of distant wildlife are the backdrop to your shared adventure. Florida's state parks offer a canvas where the verdant hues of flora and the soothing sounds of waterfalls set the stage for moments of connection and exploration.

Picture yourselves embarking on hikes that lead to panoramic vistas, discovering hidden springs that mirror the azure skies, and traversing trails that wind through ancient oak hammocks. Each step becomes a declaration of love for the outdoors and a celebration of the shared experiences that unfold in these natural sanctuaries.

As you turn the pages of this chapter, envision the joy of stumbling upon hidden gems, the thrill of reaching the summit together, and the quiet moments by the water's edge. This is an invitation to escape the familiar, to breathe in the fresh air scented with pine and cypress, and to forge memories that will linger like the echoes of a distant waterfall.

In the following pages, we'll explore the trails of love, where state parks become the playgrounds for couples seeking both serenity and adventure. Whether you're seasoned hikers or casual wanderers, Florida's state parks promise an immersive experience—a chance to reconnect not only with each other but also with the untamed beauty that defines the Sunshine State.

1. Hike in Ocala National Forest-*Recommended Cities*: Ocala,

Gainesville

Escape into the enchanting wilderness of Ocala National Forest, where numerous hiking trails await exploration. Hand in hand, you and your partner can immerse yourselves in the beauty of ancient oaks, serene lakes, and dense forests. Choose from easy, family-friendly trails to more challenging ones, all offering opportunities to observe wildlife and reconnect with nature. Don't forget to visit Juniper Springs, a crystal-clear pool that's perfect for a refreshing dip fed by artesian springs.

https://www.fs.usda.gov/recarea/florida/recarea/?recid=835
28

Free entrance

2. Corkscrew Swamp Sanctuary in Naples-*Recommended City:* Naples

Take a romantic stroll along the tranquil boardwalks of Corkscrew Swamp Sanctuary. This natural oasis is a haven for birdwatchers and nature enthusiasts. As you walk hand in hand, keep your eyes peeled for alligators, wading birds, and breathtaking cypress trees draped in Spanish moss. It's an ideal spot for couples seeking serenity and the chance to connect with Florida's unique wildlife.

https://corkscrew.audubon.org/

Admission $17

3. Kanapaha Botanical Gardens in Gainesville-*Recommended City*: Gainesville

Spend quality time together amidst the vibrant colors and fragrant blooms of Kanapaha Botanical Gardens. Meander through themed gardens, admire water lilies in the largest herbaceous water garden in the Southeast and find solace in the bamboo garden's peaceful atmosphere. This enchanting setting invites you to savor each other's company while surrounded by the beauty of nature.

https://kanapaha.org/

Admission $10

4. Paynes Prairie Preserve State Park." Located in Micanopy, Florida, Paynes Prairie is a unique and diverse natural area. It's known for its extensive wetlands, home to a wide variety of wildlife, including alligators, bison, wild horses, and numerous bird species.

Couples can explore the park through hiking and biking trails and an observation tower for panoramic views of the prairie. A visitor center also provides information about the park's ecology and history. Paynes Prairie Preserve State Park offers a chance to experience Florida's natural beauty, wildlife, nature, and romance. It's a place where couples can create special memories together while immersing themselves in the natural beauty of Florida's wilderness.

https://www.floridastateparks.org/parks-and-trails/paynes-prairie-preserve-state-park

8 am to Sundown- 365

$6 per vehicle

5. Hike in Myakka River State Park-*Recommended City*: Sarasota
Venture into the wilderness of Myakka River State Park, where various hiking trails cater to different skill levels. Share awe-inspiring moments as you stroll along trails that wind through oak hammocks,

palmetto prairies, and wetlands. For an added thrill, walk the Myakka Canopy Walkway, suspended among the trees, offering panoramic views of the park's landscapes.

Photo by Camille Robinson:
https://www.pexels.com/photo/couple-cuddling-in-a-forest-10822202/

6. Visit Big Cypress National Preserve-*Recommended City*: Naples
Embark on an adventure into the subtropical wilderness of Big Cypress National Preserve. Choose from a range of hiking trails that allow you to explore the rich biodiversity of cypress swamps and wetlands. Keep your eyes peeled for alligators, wading birds, and other wildlife. The peaceful surroundings and opportunities for wildlife encounters make this an ideal destination for nature-loving couples.
https://floridanationalparksassociation.org/big-cypress-nati onal-preserve
Free entrance

7. Loxahatchee National Wildlife Refuge-*Recommended City*: West Palm Beach
Discover the serene wetlands and cypress swamps of Loxahatchee National Wildlife Refuge. Take a leisurely hike along the refuge's scenic trails and boardwalks, where you can enjoy the sights and sounds of the local wildlife. Consider renting a canoe to paddle through the calm waters, experiencing the refuge's beauty from a different perspective.

8. Ravine Gardens State Park in Palatka-*Recommended City*: Palatka
Step into the beautifully landscaped gardens of Ravine Gardens State Park. As you walk hand in hand along the winding trails, you'll encounter stunning terraced gardens, picturesque suspension bridges, and a unique geological ravine. Enjoy the tranquil surroundings and take in the scenic beauty that this park has to offer.
https://www.floridastateparks.org/parks-and-trails/ravine-gardens-state-park
$5 per vehicle
1600 Twigg St., Palatka FL 32177

9. Bird Watching at Merritt Island National Wildlife Refuge - *Recommended City*: Titusville -Merritt Island National Wildlife Refuge is a paradise for birdwatching couples. Explore the refuge's scenic trails and the renowned Black Point Wildlife Drive to spot various bird species. The refuge's diverse habitats, including wetlands, marshes, and coastal areas, attract a multitude of waterfowl and migratory birds. Bring your binoculars and share the excitement of identifying and observing these magnificent creatures.
https://www.fws.gov/refuge/merritt-island
1987 Scrub Jay Way #32782, Titusville, FL
$5 daily pass or $80 Annual Federal Park pass

Six

Artsy Adventures

Photo by Tiến Trần: https://www.pexels.com/photo/asian-couple-with-guitar-in-park-5985573/

In the Sunshine State, art and culture unfold like a canvas, a dynamic expression of the region's diverse heritage. From the contemporary galleries of Miami to the historic theaters of St. Augustine, couples are encouraged to explore the kaleidoscope of artistic experiences that await.

Imagine strolling hand in hand through the halls of renowned museums, where each brushstroke and sculpture tells a story, or losing yourselves in the enchanting melodies of a live performance under the stars. Florida's cultural landscape becomes the backdrop for shared discoveries, where every exhibit, every note, becomes a conversation starter and a catalyst for connection.

As you delve into the upcoming pages, envision the thrill of attending a live concert together, the awe of standing before masterpieces in renowned galleries, and the shared moments of contemplation in historic cultural landmarks. This is not just a chapter of artistic appreciation; it's an exploration of the emotions, discussions, and shared inspirations that arise in the presence of creativity.

1. Art Walks in St. Augustine

• *Recommended City: St. Augustine*

St. Augustine's art walks offer couples a captivating evening of art and culture in a self-guided tour through downtown St. Augustine. Typically held on the first Friday of each month, these events turn the historic streets into an artistic showcase. As you wander from gallery to gallery, you'll have the chance to admire and discuss the diverse works of local artists. It's a unique opportunity to connect with the local art

scene and consider taking home a piece of Florida's creativity. There are free trolleys available on a continuous loop if needed.
https://www.staaa.org/art-galleries-of-st-augustine/
First Friday Art walk 5-9 pm

2. Visit the Dali Museum in St. Petersburg

- *Recommended City: St. Petersburg*

Prepare for a surreal journey as you and your partner explore The Dali Museum in St. Petersburg. If you plan your visit on Thursday evenings, you'll enjoy reduced admission fees, making it a budget-friendly cultural experience. Inside, you'll encounter the mesmerizing works of Salvador Dali, a master of surrealism. Discuss the symbolism and intrigue of his art while surrounded by thought-provoking exhibits.
https://thedali.org/about-the-museum/

Admission plus Dali Alive 360 $34

3. Historical Walking Tours in Key West

• *Recommended City: Key West*

Dive into the captivating history of Key West through a budget-friendly historical walking tour. Wander the charming streets of this historical city, visiting landmarks that tell the tale of its colorful past. Along the way, knowledgeable guides share stories of pirates, shipwrecks, and the island's unique cultural heritage. It's a romantic way to explore Key West's rich history together. Several themed tours include The Cocktail Crawl, Jimmy Buffet, Ghosts, and Gravestone. Choose one that suits your shared interests.

4. Medieval Times in Kissimmee or Orlando, Florida.

Embark on a unique and enchanting journey into the past. The moment you step through the castle's grand gates, you are transported to a world of chivalry and pageantry. Amidst the medieval decor, knights in shining armor compete in jousting tournaments, showcasing their valor and skill. As they cheer for their favored champion, couples share in the excitement and thrill of the competition. The immersive experience continues as they indulge in a sumptuous feast, feasting on hearty fare fit for lords and ladies. With the ambiance of flickering torchlight, the clashing of swords, and the thundering hooves of horses,

61

Medieval Times in Kissimmee offers couples a unique blend of history, entertainment, and an unforgettable evening together, creating lasting memories that become part of their own love story.

5. Art Basel Miami Beach - Art Public

- *Recommended City: Miami Beach*

If your visit to Miami Beach aligns with early December, seize the opportunity to explore Art Basel Miami Beach's Art Public section. This open-air exhibition features large-scale sculptures, installations, and performances. It often transforms the beach into an art lover's paradise. Engage with contemporary art in a public and budget-friendly setting, with the shimmering ocean as the backdrop. https://www.artbasel.com/miami-beach/at-the-show

December 8-10, 2023

Day ticket $75 per person

Photo by Anton Maximov : *https://www.pexels.com/photo/grayscale-photo-of-a-couple-looking-at-the-museum-12174555/*

6. Visit the Morikami Museum and Japanese Gardens

• *Recommended City: Delray Beach*

Delve into Japanese culture and art by visiting the Morikami Museum and Japanese Gardens. To save on admission costs, plan your visit on select Saturdays. This cultural gem invites you and your partner to meander through beautifully landscaped Japanese gardens, admire traditional art, and gain insights into Japan's rich heritage. It's a tranquil and educational experience that fosters appreciation for art and culture. **https://morikami.org/**

• Adults (ages 18+): $16

- Seniors (65+): $14
- Military (with ID): $14
- College Students (with ID): $12

7. Free Museum Nights in Miami

- *Recommended City: Miami*

Explore Miami's world-class museums on a budget by taking advantage of free admission nights. Institutions like the Perez Art Museum Miami (PAMM) and the Wolfsonian-FIU Museum offer scheduled evenings when you can explore their collections without paying entry fees. It's an excellent opportunity to immerse yourselves in art, culture, and history while keeping your budget intact.

https://www.pamm.org/en/

Free admission every 2nd Saturday of the month from 11 am to 3 pm

*Photo by Kha Ruxury: https://www.pexels.com/photo/monochrome-photo-o
f-a-romantic-couple-12537741/*

8. Historic Ybor City Walking Tour in Tampa

- *Recommended City: Tampa*

Discover the cultural richness of Ybor City in Tampa through an engaging and budget-friendly walking tour. As you stroll through its historic streets, you'll uncover the city's storied cigar-making heritage, vibrant Latin culture, and intriguing architecture. Consider visiting the Ybor City Museum to deepen your understanding of this unique community's history.

9. Ringling Museum Grounds in Sarasota

- *Recommended City: Sarasota*

While the Ringling Museum charges admission, you can explore its picturesque grounds, including the breathtaking Ca' d'Zan mansion, for free on Mondays. Enjoy a leisurely walk through lush gardens, marvel at the Mediterranean-style architecture, and bask in the cultural oasis the Ringling Museum offers. It's a budget-friendly way to appreciate art, architecture, and natural beauty.

https://www.ringling.org/visit/
Admission starting at $25

Seven

Cultural Chronicles

Photo by jonathan emili: https://www.pexels.com/photo/medieval-roman-catholic-cathedral-exterior-during-snowfall-6410755/

Florida's cultural landscape is as diverse as its natural beauty, offering couples an array of artistic experiences to elevate their connection. From world-class museums showcasing timeless masterpieces to concert venues resonating with melodies that stir the soul, this chapter beckons you to immerse yourselves in the enriching world of art and culture.

Imagine strolling hand in hand through galleries adorned with captivating paintings, sculptures, and artifacts. Envision the thrill of attending live performances where the notes of music dance in the air, creating a symphony of emotions that resonate between you and your partner.

Whether you're aficionados or newcomers to the world of art and music, Florida's cultural offerings promise moments of reflection, inspiration, and connection.

1. Koreshan State Park in Estero

• *Recommended City: Estero*

Koreshan State Park is a historical treasure that once served as home to the Koreshan Unity, a utopian community in the late 19th and early 20th centuries. Walk hand-in-hand through the beautifully preserved buildings and gardens. Explore unique structures such as the "Hollow Earth" globe and learn about the unconventional beliefs of its residents. The park's serene setting along the Estero River provides a peaceful backdrop for couples to immerse themselves in Florida's intriguing history.

https://www.floridastateparks.org/parks-and-trails/koreshan-state-park

$5 per vehicle

2. Solomon's Castle in Ona

• *Recommended City: Ona*

Solomon's Castle is a captivating hidden gem that combines art, creativity, and eccentricity. Sculptor Howard Solomon built this whimsical castle using recycled materials, turning it into an art lover's paradise. Take a guided tour to explore the castle's intricate details and the surrounding sculpture gardens. It's a unique and thought-provoking experience that sparks conversations and wonderment.
http://solomonscastle.com/Default.aspx
Tour Starts at $33

3. St. Augustine Lighthouse and Maritime Museum

- *Recommended City: St. Augustine*

Ascend the St. Augustine Lighthouse together for a romantic adventure with breathtaking views. After the climb, delve into the Maritime Museum to discover the maritime heritage of the area. The lighthouse grounds are also a great spot for a leisurely picnic or a romantic moment, making it an ideal destination for couples who appreciate history, culture, and a touch of adventure.

https://www.staugustinelighthouse.org/
Starting at $14.95
Sunset/Moonrise Tour with champagne and hors d'oeuvres $40

4. Coral Castle in Homestead

- *Recommended City: Homestead*

Coral Castle is a mysterious and awe-inspiring attraction created by Edward Leedskalnin. Explore this enigmatic site, featuring massive stone sculptures and structures carved entirely by hand. The intricacy

and scale of Leedskalnin's work are sure to leave you both in awe and ignite your curiosity about the secrets behind its construction.
https://coralcastle.com/
Admission $18

5. Historic Spanish Point in Osprey

• *Recommended City: Osprey*

Historic Spanish Point is a captivating outdoor museum and botanical garden that offers a glimpse into Florida's pioneer history. Meander through historical buildings, including a pioneer chapel and a reconstructed pioneer homestead. Explore lush gardens, waterfront trails, and captivating exhibits. The tranquility and educational opportunities make it an ideal setting for couples seeking to connect with both history and nature.
https://selby.org/
Admission $18

Photo by Cristina Gottardi on Unsplash

6. Tarpon Springs Sponge Docks

- *Recommended City: Tarpon Springs*

Transport yourselves to Greece by visiting the Tarpon Springs Sponge Docks. As you stroll along the waterfront, explore charming shops offering authentic Greek products. Savor the flavors of Greek cuisine at local restaurants. For a unique experience, consider taking a boat tour to witness sponge divers in action, a tradition deeply rooted in the city's heritage.

https://spongedocks.net/things-to-do-in-tarpon-springs/

7. Ancient Spanish Monastery in North Miami Beach

- *Recommended City: North Miami Beach*

Experience the timeless beauty of the Ancient Spanish Monastery, a structure with roots dating back to the 12th century in Spain. Wander through centuries-old architecture, including picturesque cloisters and chapels. Explore the peaceful gardens, and let the historical ambiance envelop you both in a journey through time and culture.

https://www.spanishmonastery.com/

Free to visit. Closed Mondays and Tuesday and for scheduled events. Please see the schedule for open times.

16711 W Dixie Hwy, North Miami Beach, FL 33160

8. Mound Key Archaeological State Park in Estero

• *Recommended City: Estero*

Reach Mound Key Archaeological State Park by hiking or kayaking to discover the remnants of ancient Calusa Indian shell mounds. As you explore the trails and mounds, you'll gain insight into the rich cultural history of the Calusa people. The park offers a blend of history and natural beauty, providing a serene and educational experience for couples.

https://stateparks.com/mound_key_archeological_state_park_in_florida.html

Free entrance

9. The Casements in Ormond Beach –

• *Recommended City: Ormond Beach –*

The Casements, once the home of John D. Rockefeller, is an elegant and historical estate that has been transformed into a cultural and civic center. Stroll through the beautifully landscaped gardens, admire the Mediterranean-style architecture, and explore the interior. You may have the opportunity to attend cultural events, art exhibits, or even enjoy a leisurely afternoon tea. This hidden gem offers couples an opportunity to connect with history, culture, and elegance in a charming seaside setting.

http://www.thecasements.net/grounds.html

25 Riverside Dr, Ormond Beach, FL 32176

Free tours - Donations accepted.

Eight

Palate Pleasures

*Photo by Nadin Sh: https://www.pexels.com/photo/young-man-and-woma
n-sitting-at-a-street-cafe-table-17963609/*

In this section, we'll list several options, proving that a limited budget doesn't have to hinder the pleasure of dining as a couple. We'll explore the art of savoring sumptuous dishes, indulging in diverse cuisines, and creating memorable dining experiences without breaking the bank. Whether you're seeking cozy cafes, charming bistros, or hidden gems off the beaten path, these budget-friendly dining options promise to provide delectable delights and strengthen your connection, all while keeping your wallet happy.

1.**The Floridian - St. Augustine, FL**: The Floridian captures the essence of St. Augustine's historic charm. This cozy eatery specializes in Southern comfort food with a modern twist. The menu features affordable delights such as Datil Pepper Shrimp, fried green tomatoes, and hearty grits. The intimate ambiance and warm service make it an ideal spot for a romantic dinner, and the outdoor seating option is perfect for couples who want to enjoy the evening breeze.

http://www.thefloridianstaug.com/#welcome-section

72 Spanish Street, St. Augustine, FL

2.Mango's Café - Miami Beach, FL: Located in the heart of vibrant Miami Beach, Mango's Café offers a taste of the Caribbean without the hefty price tag. The colorful decor and lively atmosphere create an energetic backdrop for a budget-friendly dinner date. Couples can relish authentic Cuban sandwiches, empanadas, and fresh tropical fruit juices while being entertained by live Latin music, adding an extra layer of romance to the evening.

https://mangos.com/mangos-miami-beach/

900 Ocean Drive, Miami Beach, Fl 33139

3.The Back Porch - Destin, FL: Overlooking the emerald waters of the Gulf of Mexico in Destin, The Back Porch is a hidden gem for seafood enthusiasts. This affordable seafood restaurant boasts daily specials and fresh catches of the day, ensuring couples can savor the flavors of the sea without emptying their wallets. The relaxed, beachy vibe and outdoor seating make it an idyllic spot for a romantic sunset dinner.

https://www.theback-porch.com/welcome/

1740 Scenic Highway 98, Destin, FL 32541

4.**Blue Heaven - Key West, FL**: In the heart of historic Key West, Blue Heaven is a charming and quirky eatery celebrated for its laid-back atmosphere and reasonably priced Caribbean-inspired cuisine. Couples can share a plate of their famous banana pancakes or savor dishes like Key West pink shrimp. With local musicians providing live entertainment, the restaurant radiates a magical and budget-friendly ambiance for couples.

https://blueheavenkw.com/

729 Thomas St, Key West, FL 33040

5.**The Floridian Diner - Fort Lauderdale, FL**: The Floridian Diner in Fort Lauderdale takes couples on a journey to the nostalgic era of classic American diners. This budget-friendly spot is perfect for breakfast and brunch dates. Delight in fluffy pancakes, made-to-order omelets, or corned beef hash while soaking in the retro vibes and friendly service.

http://thefloridiandiner.com/

1410 E Las Olas Blvd, Fort Lauderdale, FL 33301

Open 24/7

*Photo by Lazuardy Azhari Bacharuddin Noor: http://www.pexels.com/phot
o/grayscale-photo-of-an-elderly-couple-11926768*

6.La Segunda Central Bakery - Tampa, FL: For a taste of Cuba on a budget, head to La Segunda Central Bakery in Tampa. This historic bakery is renowned for its authentic Cuban sandwiches and delectable pastries. Couples can share a Cuban sandwich, indulge in a guava pastry, and sip on cafe con leche for an affordable yet flavorful date. The bakery's welcoming atmosphere adds to the overall charm.

https://www.lasegundabakery.com/
2512 North 15th Street, Tampa, Fl, 33605
Everyday 6am to 3pm

7. **The Salty Pelican - Fernandina Beach, FL**: *Description*: The Salty Pelican, located in Fernandina Beach, offers an affordable dining experience with stunning waterfront views. Couples can enjoy a romantic dinner on the outdoor deck overlooking the picturesque harbor. The menu features reasonably priced seafood dishes like shrimp and grits, seafood po'boys, and flavorful salads, making it an excellent choice for a seaside date night.
https://thesaltypelicanamelia.com/
12 N Front St, Fernandina Beach, FL 32034

8.**The Floribbean - Fort Myers, FL**: The Floribbean in Fort Myers seamlessly blends Florida and Caribbean flavors in a relaxed setting. Couples can savor tropical delights like conch fritters and jerk chicken at wallet-friendly prices. The colorful decor and friendly staff create a warm and inviting atmosphere, ideal for couples seeking a flavorful yet budget-conscious dining experience.
https://thefloribbean.com/
2410 Central Ave, St. Petersburg, FL 33712
Everyday 11:30 am to 9:00pm

9.**La Teresita - Tampa, FL**: La Teresita is a cherished Tampa institution known for serving mouthwatering Cuban cuisine at affordable prices. Couples can share a plate of their famous roast pork with black beans and rice, and don't forget to treat yourselves to their crispy Cuban pastries for dessert. The restaurant's warm and welcoming ambiance sets the stage for an unforgettable budget-friendly dining experience, perfect for a romantic evening.
https://www.lateresitarestaurant.com/

3246 W Columbus Dr, Tampa, FL 33607

Sun-Thurs 6:30 am to 9pm and Fri- Sat 6:30am to midnight

Nine

Food Truck Frolic

Photo by Brett Sayles: https://www.pexels.com/photo/grayscale-photograph-of-two-people-standing-in-front-of-food-truck-1264937/

Please Note: This list could potentially change after the production of this book, however you can mark your calendars with the yearly on Florida Food Trucks.
https://www.floridafoodtrucks.com/food-truck-festivals/

You can also use the Food Truck finder app for short notice cravings on Foodie Truck
https://www.myfoodietruck.com/

1.Lake Eola Food Truck Bazaar - Eustis, FL: Nestled in the cozy town of Eustis, the Lake Eola Food Truck Bazaar is a monthly gathering of food trucks, offering an array of affordable and delectable dishes. Couples can embark on a culinary adventure with choices ranging from savory BBQ to gourmet sandwiches and creative desserts. Enjoy your meal in a relaxed atmosphere, perfect for a romantic evening in this charming small town. The tranquil lakeside setting adds an extra layer of romance to the ambiance. The picturesque backdrop of Lake Eola and its lush surroundings create a serene atmosphere, making it the perfect setting for a romantic evening with your loved one. You'll have the option to dine at picnic tables, spread a blanket by the water's edge, or even enjoy your meal under the starry night sky, ensuring that you'll find a cozy spot to savor your food together. To enhance the festive atmosphere, live music and entertainment are often part of the experience, filling the air with joyful melodies that will have you and your partner tapping your feet and perhaps even sharing a dance. The Lake Eola Food Truck Bazaar isn't just about food; it's a community gathering. This is an opportunity to connect with locals and fellow food enthusiasts, fostering a sense of togetherness that adds an extra layer of enjoyment to your evening.

2.Food Truck Rally at Mount Dora - Mount Dora, FL: Mount Dora's Food Truck Rally is a delightful event that takes place in this picturesque town. Couples can indulge in a variety of budget-friendly dishes, including artisanal hot dogs, wood-fired pizza, and mouthwatering desserts. The tranquil ambiance of Mount Dora adds an extra layer of romance to your food truck date night. Typically scheduled in the evening, the event allows you and your partner to witness the breathtaking sunset over the tranquil landscapes of Mount Dora, casting a warm, golden glow over the town. As night falls, the soft glow of twinkling lights creates a magical atmosphere, ensuring that this event is truly enchanting. So, whether you're celebrating a special occasion or simply seeking a unique date night, the Food Truck Rally in Mount Dora promises a memorable evening filled with flavor, romance, and the heartwarming spirit of the community. Enjoy a delicious journey and create cherished memories with your loved one in the charming setting of Mount Dora."

3.Food Truck Invasion - Vero Beach, FL: Vero Beach's Food Truck Invasion is a weekly culinary gathering featuring a diverse selection of food trucks. Couples can share affordable meals like seafood tacos, handcrafted burgers, and delightful sweet treats while enjoying the coastal charm of this laid-back town.

4.Food Truck Friday - Ocala, FL: Ocala's Food Truck Friday is a beloved local tradition. Couples can relish budget-friendly dishes, such as gourmet grilled cheese sandwiches, mouthwatering tacos, and refreshing ice cream treats. The event offers a friendly, family-oriented atmosphere and a taste of Ocala's vibrant food truck scene.

5.DeLand Food Truck Rally - DeLand, FL: DeLand's Food Truck Rally is a monthly celebration of food trucks, offering a diverse culinary experience. Couples can dine on a budget with options like gourmet mac 'n' cheese, wood-fired pizza, and international cuisine. Enjoy your meal in the heart of DeLand's charming and laid-back ambiance.

6.Food Trucks On The Square- Port St Lucie, Fl: This Bi- monthly gathering where couples can explore a delightful array of culinary offerings. Savor budget-friendly meals such as BBQ delights, seafood creations, a variety of ethnic cuisine and mouthwatering desserts in the welcoming atmosphere of this up and coming town. Enjoy your food with some live music. So bring a blanket or some chairs for low-budget evening out.

Every 1st and 3rd Friday of the month from 5-9pm.

7.Sanford Food Truck Fiesta - Sanford, FL: Sanford's Food Truck Fiesta is a regular event that brings together food trucks offering a wide range of flavors. Couples can enjoy affordable dishes like Cuban sandwiches, gourmet sliders, and sweet treats in the heart of Sanford's historic and picturesque town.

https://www.historicdowntownsanford.com/events/sanford-food-truck-fiesta/

Every 3rd Saturday from 1-6pm

*Photo by Tima Miroshnichenko: https://www.pexels.com/photo/people-stan
ding-near-a-food-truck-5794160/*

8.Food Truck Roundup - Jupiter, FL: Jupiter's Food Truck Roundup is a recurring event that invites couples to savor budget-friendly meals. Explore a variety of culinary delights, including tacos, wood-fired pizza, and artisanal sandwiches, all while enjoying the coastal charm of this quaint town.

9.Food Truck Invasion - Sebastian, FL: Sebastian hosts the Food Truck Invasion, a community event featuring an assortment of food trucks. Couples can share affordable dishes like gourmet hot dogs, fresh lobster rolls, and savory crepes while soaking in the relaxed coastal atmosphere of this charming town.

10.River City Food Truck Festival- Debary, FL.. This charming event is a perfect destination for couples seeking a unique and flavorful date night. Situated in the heart of DeBary, it offers a chance to savor a wide variety of delectable dishes served by a diverse array of food trucks, creating an enchanting evening filled with gastronomic delights and community spirit.As you stroll through the event, you'll be greeted by a symphony of tempting aromas and a colorful array of gourmet offerings from the many food trucks in attendance. From savory delights to sweet indulgences, you and your partner can savor everything from gourmet burgers to artisanal tacos, wood-fired pizza to mouthwatering desserts. With such a diverse selection, there's something to satisfy every palate.

11.Merritt Island Food Truck Festival- Merritt Island, FL. Nestled in the heart of Merritt Island, Florida, this vibrant event is a paradise for foodies and a perfect setting for couples looking to embark on a flavorful adventure. This food truck festival showcases an eclectic array of culinary delights, from savory to sweet, served up by a diverse lineup of food trucks. You and your partner can savor gourmet burgers, indulge in artisanal tacos, enjoy wood-fired pizza, and cap it all off with delectable desserts. With so many options, you're sure to find a dish that tickles your taste buds.

https://www.facebook.com/events/511511504459676/516178047326355/

Every last Sunday 1-6pm

12.Discover Culinary Delights: Wednesday Food Trucks in Volunteer Park, Plantation, FL. Indulge in a delightful midweek escape with your partner at Volunteer Park's renowned Wednesday Food Trucks event. Nestled in the heart of the city, this weekly gathering promises a mouthwatering journey through a vibrant tapestry of flavors that will leave you and your significant other craving for more.

• Culinary Adventure: Explore an array of delectable options from a diverse lineup of food trucks. From gourmet burgers to artisanal tacos, wood-fired pizza to sweet treats, there's something to satisfy every craving. Each truck is a culinary gem, offering a unique taste experience.

- Scenic Ambiance: Volunteer Park, with its lush greenery and tranquil surroundings, sets the perfect backdrop for a romantic outing. The majestic views of the park's iconic water tower and beautiful landscaping create a serene atmosphere for couples to unwind and connect.

- Live Entertainment: As you savor your favorite dishes, enjoy the rhythmic beats of live music and entertainment that infuse the park with energy. The sounds of local musicians and performers add to the festive atmosphere. Community Vibes: The Wednesday Food Trucks at Volunteer Park have become a beloved community gathering. Couples can mingle with friendly locals and fellow food enthusiasts, fostering a sense of togetherness that enhances the experience.

- Evening Magic: The event starts in the late afternoon and extends into the evening, allowing you to relish the beautiful sunset with your partner while enjoying your delicious meals. The soft glow of twinkling lights creates a magical atmosphere as night falls.

- Ample Seating: Plenty of seating options, from picnic tables to cozy blankets on the grass, make it easy for couples to find a comfortable spot to enjoy their meals while taking in the view. Supporting Local: By dining at the food trucks, you're not only treating yourselves to fantastic food but also supporting local vendors and the community. So, whether you're celebrating a special occasion or simply looking for a unique midweek date night, Wednesday Food Trucks at Volunteer Park promises a memorable experience filled with flavor, romance, and community spirit. Create lasting memories with your loved one, one delicious bite at a time!

https://www.facebook.com/FoodTruckWednesdays/

12050 W Sunrise Blvd, Plantation, FL 33323-2231, United States,

Ten

Sunset and Stargazing

Photo by Yan Krukau: https://www.pexels.com/photo/a-couple-sanding-on-bach-rocks-5479849/

In the vast expanse of Florida's skies, a chapter of celestial serenity awaits couples seeking moments of wonder and tranquility. As the sun dips below the horizon and the stars emerge to sprinkle the night canvas, this chapter unfolds as a cosmic playground—a place where shared gazes upward become a timeless dance with the universe. Imagine standing hand in hand, your silhouettes outlined by the fiery glow of the setting sun, the waves whispering secrets along the shoreline. As day transitions to night, envision finding a secluded spot, far from city lights, where the brilliance of the stars takes center stage, igniting conversations about constellations, galaxies, and the infinite possibilities that stretch beyond.

1.**Beach Picnic - Siesta Key, FL**: Siesta Key is renowned for its mesmerizing sunsets over the Gulf of Mexico. Create a memorable evening by packing a delightful picnic with your favorite snacks and drinks. Find a secluded spot on the soft, powdery sand, and witness the sun's majestic descent beneath the horizon. Stay awhile after sunset to stargaze, as the unspoiled skies in this tranquil town provide an exceptional view of the night sky.

2.**Sunset Cruise - Key Largo, FL**: Key Largo offers captivating sunsets over the ocean, and there's no better way to experience them than on a serene cruise. While a private sunset cruise may be on the pricier side, you can still embark on a remarkable and romantic journey by joining a group boat tour. As the sun paints the sky with vivid colors, you and your partner can bask in the tranquil ambiance and create cherished memories.

3.**State Park Stargazing - Big Pine Key, FL**: *Description*: Bahia Honda State Park on Big Pine Key beckons couples with its breathtaking sunsets and exceptional stargazing opportunities. Bring a blanket, settle on the beach, and be mesmerized by the sunset's beauty. As the night unfolds, the park's secluded location offers minimal light pollution, providing an unobstructed view of the celestial wonders above. Discover constellations, shooting stars, and the Milky Way as you stargaze hand in hand.

4.**Sunset at Clearwater Beach - Clearwater, FL**: Clearwater Beach is renowned for its awe-inspiring sunsets, and the simple act of strolling along the sandy shoreline is enough to create a magical evening. As the sun gracefully dips below the horizon, the beach's serene atmosphere sets the stage for a romantic sunset experience. Stay awhile to savor the starlit skies, as the town's coastal setting ensures a perfect backdrop for stargazing.

5.**Lovers Key State Park - Fort Myers Beach, FL**: Lovers Key State Park, nestled in Fort Myers Beach, offers a romantic and natural setting for couples to enjoy the sunset and stargazing. Pack a picnic, witness the sun's descent over the Gulf of Mexico, and relish the tranquil ambiance. As darkness envelops the park, the absence of city lights enhances the stargazing experience, making it an ideal location to admire the brilliance of the night sky together.

*Photo by Polina Tankilevitch: https://www.pexels.com/photo/couple-standi
ng-together-under-bright-sky-7741660/*

6.**Sunset at Naples Pier - Naples, FL**: Naples Pier is an iconic spot for sunset viewing. While Naples exudes luxury, the simple pleasure of strolling along the pier to watch the sunset is accessible to all. After the sun's dazzling display, extend your evening by lying on the sandy shore and gazing at the stars. The clear skies above the Gulf of Mexico provide an excellent canvas for identifying constellations and celestial wonders.

7.**Myakka River State Park - Sarasota, FL**: Myakka River State Park in Sarasota offers an inviting natural environment for couples. Arrive before sunset to explore the park's beauty and find a secluded spot to witness the sun's grandeur. Afterward, spread out a blanket and immerse yourselves in the serenity of stargazing. The park's remote location minimizes light pollution, allowing you to enjoy the night sky's celestial splendor.

8.**Beach Bonfire - Vero Beach, FL**: Vero Beach permits beach bonfires, creating a magical setting for couples. As the sun sets, kindle a bonfire and savor the warmth while roasting marshmallows for s'mores. The sound of the waves and the soft glow of the fire set the stage for a deeply romantic evening, perfect for stargazing as the night sky unfolds its brilliance above.

9.**Sunset at Cocoa Beach Pier - Cocoa Beach, FL**: Cocoa Beach Pier is a timeless destination for watching the sunset over the Atlantic Ocean. Enjoy a leisurely walk along the pier as the sun paints the sky with vibrant hues. After sunset, find a cozy spot on the beach to continue your evening with stargazing. The serene sounds of the waves create an idyllic atmosphere for your nighttime celestial exploration.

10.Honeymoon Island State Park - Dunedin, FL: Honeymoon Island State Park, located near Dunedin, offers a peaceful and secluded setting for couples. Revel in the beauty of the sunset on the beach, and as the night descends, lay out a comfortable blanket for stargazing. The park's location, far from the glare of city lights, provides an exceptional opportunity to appreciate the awe-inspiring wonders of the night sky together.

Eleven

Homely Hearts

Photo by Tima Miroshnichenko: *https://www.pexels.com/photo/grayscale-photo-of-a-couple-baking-together-5834739/*

In the hustle and bustle of daily life, it's easy for the spark in a relationship to dim. Work, responsibilities, and the demands of the world can often take precedence over nurturing the connection between two people deeply in love. Yet, the key to keeping the flame alive lies not in grand gestures or extravagant escapades, but in the simple, intimate moments shared within the comfort of your own home. In this section, we explore the art of rekindling romance in the most familiar of settings. From cooking up culinary delights together to immersing yourselves in the world of film, from playful game nights to heartfelt conversations, these activities are designed to ignite the passion and strengthen the bond between couples. It's a reminder that, even amidst life's chaos, love can flourish within the walls of your home, and the smallest moments can rekindle the spark that initially brought you together."

These activities provide opportunities to nurture your relationship, create lasting memories, and reignite the spark between you and your partner. Whether it's through shared laughter, romantic moments, or deep conversations, these experiences can help you grow closer as a couple.

1. Cook Together: Cooking together can be an enjoyable and intimate experience. You can take turns choosing recipes, shopping for ingredients, and creating delicious meals from scratch. Whether you're experimenting with international cuisines or perfecting your favorite comfort foods, the shared effort in the kitchen fosters teamwork and communication. As you savor the fruits of your labor, the satisfaction of a job well done and the joy of sharing a meal will bring you closer.

2. Movie Night: A home movie night is more than just entertainment; it's a chance to snuggle up and bond over shared cinematic experiences. You can curate a diverse selection of films, from classic love stories to action-packed adventures. The atmosphere of your own living room provides comfort and privacy, allowing you to relax and let the emotions of the movies wash over you. Don't forget the popcorn, blankets, and a bottle of your favorite wine or beverage to make the evening even cozier.

3. Game Night: Game night offers the perfect blend of competition, fun, and quality time. You can dust off classic board games like Chess, Scrabble, or Risk, or try more modern favorites like Settlers of Catan or Ticket to Ride. Card games such as Poker, Uno, or even a friendly game of Go Fish can also provide hours of amusement. The laughter, strategy, and shared moments of triumph or defeat can create lasting memories and strengthen your connection.

4. Home Spa Night: Create an oasis of relaxation in your own home with a spa night. Draw a warm bath, add some fragrant bath salts, and enjoy a leisurely soak together. Light scented candles, put on soothing music, and take turns giving each other massages with scented oils. The calming ambiance and physical intimacy will help you both unwind and reconnect on a deeper level.

5. Write Love Letters: Handwritten love letters are a timeless way to express your feelings and deepen your emotional connection. Take some time to reflect on what you adore about each other and what you dream of for your future together. These letters become cherished keepsakes, serving as beautiful reminders of your love for one another.

Photo by the Shaan photography: *https://www.pexels.com/photo/grayscale-photo-of-a-couple-smiling-while-sitting-15084942/*

6. Dance Together: Dancing at home is not just a playful activity; it's a chance to let your hair down and celebrate your love through movement. Put on your favorite songs and dance like nobody's watching. Whether you prefer slow and romantic waltzes or spontaneous and energetic dance-offs, it's a fantastic way to be in sync, have fun, and build a deeper connection.

7. **Plan a Future Vacation**: Planning a future vacation together is not only exciting but also a wonderful opportunity to align your dreams and aspirations. Discussing destinations, accommodations, and activities can help you both discover shared interests and cultivate a sense of anticipation. This activity is a chance to nurture your dreams and strengthen your partnership.

8. **DIY Project**: Tackling a DIY project together can be an adventure in teamwork. Whether it's a home improvement task, creating custom artwork, or building furniture, the shared sense of accomplishment can be deeply rewarding. This collaborative effort will not only enhance your home but also strengthen your bond.

9. Book Club for Two: Reading together allows you to share an intellectual and emotional journey. Select a book you both want to read, set a reading schedule, and then engage in conversations about the characters, plot, and themes. It's a unique way to connect on a deeper level and experience the magic of storytelling together.

10. Stargazing: Stargazing offers an opportunity to connect with the cosmos and with each other. On a clear night, set up a comfortable spot outside, whether it's on your balcony, in your backyard, or simply on a blanket on the living room floor. Gaze at the stars, identify constellations, and marvel at the beauty of the night sky. It's a serene and contemplative activity that invites heartfelt conversations and quiet moments of wonder.

These activities provide opportunities for couples to revive their relationship and rediscover the spark in the comfort of their own home. By sharing these moments, you not only deepen your connection but also create lasting memories that continue to ignite your love.

Photo by Laura Garcia from Pexels: https://www.pexels.com/photo/loving-hispanic-couple-hugging-near-wooden-wall-4924911/

Twelve

Conclusion

In concluding our journey through "Florida Couples Adventure: 100 Budget-Friendly Attractions, Activities, and Restaurants for Two," we celebrate the countless shared moments, laughter, and discoveries that have undoubtedly enriched your love story. This guide was crafted with the intention of transforming ordinary days into extraordinary adventures, proving that creating lasting memories with your partner need not come with a hefty price tag.

As you close this book, consider it not just a guide but a companion that encouraged you to explore, connect, and savor the diverse offerings of Florida's vibrant landscapes. Whether you found yourselves immersed in the cultural tapestry of historic districts, basking in the beauty of sunset beach walks, or delighting in the flavors of budget-friendly dining, every experience was an opportunity to deepen your connection and celebrate the unique bond you share. I hope you utilize the free space to document dates and thoughts from your time together.

May the adventures continue, both within the pages of this guide and beyond, as you and your partner embark on a journey of love, exploration, and shared discoveries. Here's to many more budget-friendly escapades and the enduring joy of being each other's favorite adventure buddy. Safe travels and abundant love on your Florida couples adventure!

Thirteen

References

Ancient Spanish Monastery. (n.d.). Spanish Monastery. Retrieved October 12, 2023, from https://www.spanishmonastery.com/

Audubon Corkscrew Swamp Sanctuary. (n.d.). Audubon Corkscrew Swamp Sanctuary. Retrieved October 5, 2023, from https://corkscrew.audubon.org/

Big Cypress National Preserve - Florida National Parks Association. (2023, September 18). Florida National Parks Association. Retrieved October 5, 2023, from https://floridanationalparksassociation.org/big-cypress-national-preserve

Blue Heaven Key West. (n.d.). Retrieved October 16, 2023, from https://blueheavenkw.com/

Coral Castle Museum. (n.d.). Retrieved October 10, 2023, from https://coralcastle.com/

Facebook. (n.d.-a). Retrieved October 18, 2023, from https://www.facebook.com/thefoodtruckbazaar/

Facebook. (n.d.-b). Retrieved October 19, 2023, from https://www.facebook.com/events/511511504459676/516178047326355/

Facebook. (n.d.-c). Retrieved October 20, 2023, from https://www.fa cebook.com/FoodTruckWednesdays/

First Friday Art Walk. (n.d.). Retrieved October 6, 2023, from https://www.staaa.org/art-galleries-of-st-augustine/

Florida Food Trucks. (2023, October 17). *Florida Food Truck Festivals & Events 2023 | Florida Food Trucks*. Florida Food Trucks |. https://ww w.floridafoodtrucks.com/food-truck-festivals/

Foodie Truck - Finding food trucks near you just got easy! (n.d.). Retrieved October 17, 2023, from https://www.myfoodietruck.com/

Gress, A. (2023, October 12). *Home - St Augustine Light House*. St Augustine Light House. Retrieved October 10, 2023, from https://ww w.staugustinelighthouse.org/

Historic Downtown Sanford. (2021, August 7). *Sanford Food Truck Fiesta - historic downtown Sanford*. Retrieved October 19, 2023, from https://www.historicdowntownsanford.com/events/sanford-food-tru ck-fiesta/

Home | La Teresita. (n.d.). La Teresita. Retrieved October 18, 2023, from https://www.lateresitarestaurant.com/

HOME | new-big-cypress. (n.d.). New-big-cypress. Retrieved October 2, 2023, from https://www.bigcypressswampbuggytours.com/

Home page. (n.d.). Retrieved October 17, 2023, from http://thefloridi andiner.com/

Horseback Beach Ride | Fort Pierce, FL - Tours on horseback. (n.d.). Retrieved September 14, 2023, from http://www.beachtoursonhor seback.com/

Hot Air Balloon Flight | Air Hound Adventures | Florida. (n.d.). AirHoundFL. Retrieved October 4, 2023, from https://www.airh oundfl.com/

IFLY Indoor Skydiving | You Can Fly | Locations nationwide. (2023, November 1). iFLY Holdings, Inc. Retrieved September 21, 2023, from https://www.iflyworld.com/

Kissimmee Go-Karts Bookings. (n.d.). Kissimmee Go-Karts. Retrieved September 21, 2023, from https://www.kissimmeegokarts.com

Koreshan State Park. (n.d.). Florida State Parks. Retrieved October 9, 2023, from https://www.floridastateparks.org/parks-and-trails/koreshan-state-park

La segunda Bakery in Tampa Bay | Est. 1915. (n.d.). La Segunda Bakery in Tampa Bay | Est. 1915. Retrieved October 17, 2023, from https://www.lasegundabakery.com/

Lake Kissimmee State Park. (n.d.). Florida State Parks. Retrieved October 3, 2023, from https://www.floridastateparks.org/parks-and-trails/lake-kissimmee-state-park

Lido Key Kayaking Tours - Kayaking SRQ. (n.d.). Kayaking SRQ. Retrieved September 14, 2023, from https://kayakingsrq.com/kayaking-tours/

Mango's Tropical Cafe. (2023, November 9). *Night Club, Dinner, & Show Venue In Miami, FL | Mango's Tropical Café.* Mangos.com | a Nightclub, Restaurant, Dinner and Show, Live Music and Private Events Venue. Retrieved October 15, 2023, from https://mangos.com/mangos-miami-beach/

Marie Selby Botanical Gardens. (2023, November 6). *Marie Selby Botanical Gardens - The Living Museum.* Retrieved October 11, 2023, from https://selby.org/

Merritt Island National Wildlife Refuge | U.S. Fish & Wildlife Service. (2023, November 1). FWS.gov. Retrieved October 7, 2023, from https://www.fws.gov/refuge/merritt-island

Merritt Island Wildlife Association | U.S. Fish & Wildlife Service. (n.d.). FWS.gov. Retrieved September 19, 2023, from https://www.fws.gov/partner/merritt-island-wildlife-association

Miami-Dade County Online Services. (n.d.). *Haulover Park - Miami-Dade County.* https://www.miamidade.gov/parks/haulover.asp

Morikami Museum and Japanese Gardens. (n.d.). Morikami Museum and Japanese Gardens. Retrieved October 8, 2023, from https://morik ami.org/

National Forests in Florida - Ocala National Forest. (n.d.). Retrieved October 4, 2023, from https://www.fs.usda.gov/recarea/florida/recar ea/?recid=83528

Orlando. (n.d.). Andretti Indoor Karting & Games. Retrieved October 3, 2023, from https://andrettikarting.com/orlando

Paddle Boarding Palm Beach • Paddle Boarding Palm Beach. (2023, May 25). Paddle Boarding Palm Beach. Retrieved September 15, 2023, from https://paddleboardingpalmbeach.com/

Paynes Prairie Preserve State Park. (n.d.). Florida State Parks. Retrieved October 5, 2023, from https://www.floridastateparks.org/parks-and-t rails/paynes-prairie-preserve-state-park

Pérez Art Museum Miami. (2023, November 7). *Pérez Art Museum Miami • PAMM.* Retrieved November 8, 2023, from https://www.pam m.org/en/

Ravine Gardens State Park. (n.d.). Florida State Parks. Retrieved October 6, 2023, from https://www.floridastateparks.org/parks-and-t rails/ravine-gardens-state-park

Shell Key Shuttle. (n.d.). Retrieved September 20, 2023, from https://s hellkeyshuttle.com/

Siesta Key Crystal Classic | Sand Sculpting Festival. (n.d.). Siesta Key Crystal Classic. Retrieved September 13, 2023, from https://www.sies takeycrystalclassic.com/

Solomon's Castle. (n.d.). Retrieved October 9, 2023, from http://solo monscastle.com/Default.aspx

Tarpon Springs Sponge Docks. (2023, July 14). *Things to do in Tarpon Springs - Tarpon Springs Sponge Docks.* Retrieved October 11, 2023, from https://spongedocks.net/things-to-do-in-tarpon-springs/

The Casements - Ormond Beach, Florida. (n.d.). Retrieved October 14, 2023, from http://www.thecasements.net/grounds.html

The Floribbean. (2023, September 21). *Caribbean Food in St. Pete |*
Floribbean. The FLORIBBEAN Eatery and Catering. Retrieved October
17, 2023, from https://thefloribbean.com/

The Floridian. (n.d.). The Floridian. Retrieved October 14, 2023, from
http://www.thefloridianstaug.com/#welcome-section

The Musuem. (n.d.). Dali Alive 360. Retrieved October 7, 2023, from
https://thedali.org/about-the-museum/

The Ringling Museum. (2023, September 5). *Visit - The Ringling*. The
Ringling. Retrieved October 9, 2023, from https://www.ringling.org/v
isit/

The Salty Pelican - Seafood Bar and Grill - Fernandina Beach Amelia
Island. (2022, July 7). The Salty Pelican. Retrieved October 17, 2023,
from https://thesaltypelicanamelia.com/

TheBackPorch. (n.d.). theBackPorch. Retrieved October 15, 2023,
from https://www.theback-porch.com/welcome/

Treasure Coast Sailing Adventures | South FL Boat Tours | Sailing trip.
(n.d.). Treasure Coast Sailing Adventures. https://www.treasurecoasts
ailingadventures.com/

Unforgettable Nature experiences. (n.d.). Get Your Guide. Retrieved
September 18, 2023, from https://www.getyourguide.com

Visitor information. (n.d.). Art Basel. Retrieved October 7, 2023, from
https://www.artbasel.com/miami-beach/at-the-show

Walker, T. (n.d.). *Mound Key Archeological State Park*. State Parks.
Retrieved October 13, 2023, from https://stateparks.com/mound_key
_archeological_state_park_in_florida.html

Wdd. (n.d.). *Gatorland*. Retrieved September 20, 2023, from https://w
ww.gatorland.com/

Wdd. (2023, July 31). *TreeHoppers Aerial Adventure Park near Tampa*
| Zip Line Ropes Course | Dade City, FL. Treehoppers | Just Another
WordPress Site. Retrieved October 3, 2023, from https://treehoppers.c
om/

Zoocru: zoocru.com. (n.d.). *Florida Airboat Rides at Gator Park - Everglades Airboat Tours, Everglades National Park Florida Tours, Miami Everglades Tours, Everglades Airboat Rides, Florida Everglades Airboat Tours.* GATOR PARK. https://www.gatorpark.com/

Fourteen

Appendix

North Florida
Amelia Island
Cape San Blas
Daytona Beach
Destin
Eustis
Fernandina
Gainesville
Jacksonville
Micanopy
Ormond Beach
Palatka
Panama City
Pensacola
St Augustine

Central Florida
  Brooksville
  Clearwater Beach
  Clermont
  Cocoa Beach
  Dade City
  Debary
  DeLand
  Dunedin
  Fort Pierce
  Hutchinson Island
  Kissimmee
  Merritt Island
  Mount Dora
  Ocala
  Ona
  Orlando
  Osprey
  Sanford
  Sarasota
  St Petersburg
  Tampa
  Tarpon Springs
  Titusville

South Florida
  Big Pine Key
  Captiva Island
  Chokoloskee
  Coral Gables
  Delray Beach

Estero
Fort Lauderdale
Fort Myers
Fort Myers Beach
Hollywood
Homestead
Jupiter
Key Largo
Key West
Miami
Naples
North Miami Beach
Oakland Park
Plantation
Port St Lucie
Sanibel Island
Sebastian
Shell Island
Stuart
Vero Beach
West Palm Beach

About the Author

Abigail enjoys being in nature! Gardening and new animal encounters are her favorite. Her recent accomplishments are starting Abbysmicrogreens.com, and a small book-publishing company. This is the second book in the Florida travel adventure series.

Also by Abigail Skerritt-Jones

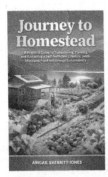

JOURNEY TO HOMESTEAD: A Practical Guide to Transitioning, Thriving and Sustaining a Self-Sufficient Lifestyle, while Managing Food and Energy Sustainability

Discover step-by-step guides to crafting functional chicken coops, beekeeping setups, and more to elevate your self-sufficient lifestyle.

Turn kitchen scraps and yard trimmings into "black gold" using foolproof methods for nutrient-rich compost creation.

Embrace nature's harmony by harnessing natural pest control methods, ensuring your crops remain pristine without harmful chemicals.

Explore various preservation techniques, from the traditional art of pickling to modern freezing and fermentation methods.

Embark on a journey of herbalism, cultivating and utilizing medicinal plants to foster health and well-being for your family.

FLORIDA
FAMILY
ADVENTURES
100 BUDGET-FRIENDLY ACTIVITIES
FOR KIDS AND FAMILIES
BY ABIGAIL SKERRITT-JONES

Florida Family Adventures : 100 Budget-Friendly Activities for Kids and Families
"Do you want to make amazing memories with your kids and family in Florida but don't want to spend a fortune? Here are 100 Unforgettable Experiences that Won't Break the Bank!"

Quality family time shouldn't come at a sky-high price. What if you could unlock the hidden gems of Florida that are both top-notch and wallet-friendly?

"I'm bored!" Sound familiar? Bid farewell to boredom with a colossal collection of 100 ingenious activities that'll keep your kids engaged and entertained.